GET YOUR HEAD OUT OF YOUR ASSETS

Turn Your Valuable Assets into Charitable Gifts

(An Illustrated Guide)

Patricia A. Guter J.D., CFP®

Illustrated by Christina Escamilla

Dedication

Get Your Head Out of Your Assets is dedicated to all individuals and organizations that want to make a positive difference in their community, their country, and around the world.

And to my husband Don and my daughters Kerry and Kelly, thank you for always caring about others and believing in me.

CONTENTS

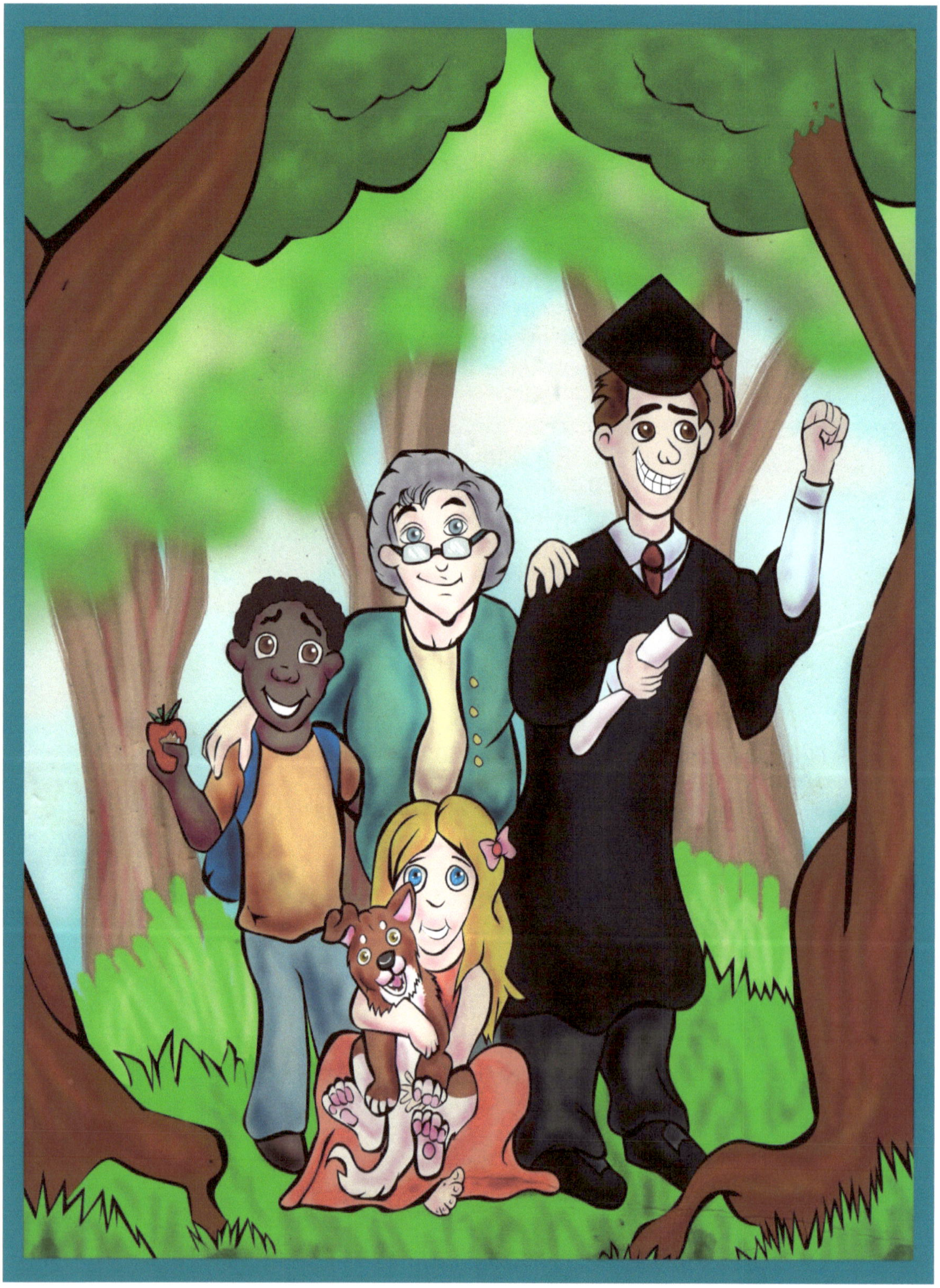

FOREWORD

It is estimated that less than 10% of our nation's wealth is in cash and over 90% is in non-cash assets.[1]

Assets are items that are owned and have value; the entries on a balance sheet showing the items of property owned, including cash, inventory, equipment, real estate, accounts receivable and goodwill; and all the property of a person (including a bankrupt or deceased person) available for paying debts or for distribution. [2]

Get Your Head Out of Your Assets is written for people who want to make a difference. Everyone cares about something—promoting better health and education, combating poverty, and conserving nature, animals, and the environment. There are too many charitable causes and services to list. However, with your passion and commitment to the cause of your choice, you can and will make a positive change in the lives of those in your community, country, and around the world.

Get Your Head Out of Your Assets is for individuals and organizations that are morally committed to a charitable cause and want to provide charitable support for those in need. Charitable gift planning (planned gifts), tools, and techniques can be the solution to making a sustainable commitment in supporting charitable initiatives and missions. Converting your assets into charitable gifts can make a difference and enable change to take place for a better world.

---

[1] PlannedGiving.com, summer 2014, p.8.
[2] Black's Law Dictionary 140 (10th ed. 2014).

i

With Your Passion and Commitment to the Cause of Your Choice, You Will Make a Positive Change in Our World!

NONPROFIT TAX-EXEMPT ORGANIZATIONS NEED PROFITS TO REACH PHILANTHROPIC AND HUMANITARIAN GOALS

Nonprofit tax-exempt organizations (charities) need profits (earnings greater than expenses) to remain sustainable in order to reach their philanthropic and humanitarian goals. Charities can and do make profits (through gifts, grants, etc.) but the profits must be used solely for their operation, administration, and mission, or in the case of foundations, granted to other nonprofit tax-exempt organizations for their operation, administration, and mission.

Charities cannot use their funds for anything other than the mission for which they were formed. Even when a charity goes out of business, its remaining assets must be given to another similarly purposed charity to further that charity's mission. In contrast, when a for-profit organization goes out of business, its assets can be liquidated and the proceeds distributed to the owners or the shareholders. Nonprofit tax-exempt organizations (charities) do not have owners or shareholders. They have a charitable mission.

To better appreciate and understand the term nonprofit tax-exempt organization, let us look at the meaning of each word. The terms nonprofit and tax-exempt represent different state and federal laws regulating charities.

Nonprofit status is a state law concept and is determined by each individual state. Nonprofit status may allow the organization to qualify for benefits at the state level, including exemption from state and local sales, property, and income taxes. Registering as a nonprofit at the state level does not automatically result in tax-exemption at the federal level. At the federal level, tax-exempt status for a charitable organization is determined by the Internal Revenue Service (IRS) under the Internal Revenue Code (IRC) §501. A tax-exempt organization, for example, a charity, by law, is not subject to federal taxation. In addition, IRS recognized §501(c)(3) organizations have the ability to apply for grants and other public or private charitable allocations.

For more information on IRC §501(c) organizations, explore the IRS website www.irs.gov.[3]

Before deciding to support a charity, it is always prudent to be familiar with the organization, its administration, and philanthropic goals. Keep in mind that most people give to a charitable cause because they care about what the charity does. They feel that through the charity, they can make a difference in their community, their country, and the world. Everyone can make a difference through charitable giving.

Gathering and preserving financial support for charitable organizations can be challenging. Nonprofit tax-exempt entities (charities) rely on private charitable gifts, contributions, and the income from them to remain sustainable. Moral, financial, and philanthropic generosity support nonprofit tax-exempt entities, enabling them to remain strong, allowing them to achieve their charitable goals. Not only will the charities benefit from financial and philanthropic support, but financial and philanthropic support of a charity can offer significant personal financial and estate planning opportunities for a donor.

Personal financial and estate planning opportunities may include but are not limited to:

- An increase in income achieved by charitable gifting strategies, such as charitable gift annuities and charitable trusts.

- An income tax charitable deduction, which may reduce a donor's taxable income (as allowed by law).

---

[3] Charities-&-Non-Profits/Charitable-Organizations/Exemption-Requirements-Section-501(c) (3) Organizations, http://www.irs.gov.

- An avoidance of capital gains tax on the transfer of appreciated assets to a charity.

- A reduction of estate taxes and/or probate costs (as allowed by law).

Often, donors find that giving is its own reward.
Now Get Your Head Out of Your Assets and Make a Difference!

CHARITABLE GIFTING STRATEGIES

A GIFT OF CASH

Cash is money or its equivalent. Cash includes paper currency, coins, negotiable checks, balances in bank accounts, electronic funds transfers, and debit and credit card transactions.

🎁 Plan a Gift:

- Cash contributions may be designated by the donor for a charity's specific program, or may be undesignated. An undesignated contribution makes a gift available for a charity's most pressing needs, as determined by the charity.

Benefits to a Donor:

- A gift of cash is simple, common, and convenient.

- A charitable deduction may reduce taxable income (as allowed by law).

- Charitable deductions are eligible up to 50% of adjusted gross income (AGI) in a given year.

- If charitable deductions exceed 50% of adjusted gross income in a given year, the donor may carry the excess deductions on their income tax returns up to five additional years if eligible.

- The higher the donor's tax rate, the more the donor will usually save from a charitable deduction.

- An itemized deduction phase-out for higher income taxpayers may occur, but state taxes, mortgage interest, and other common deductions will normally absorb these reductions whether or not charitable gifts are made. [4]

Benefits to a Charity:

- A gift of cash is simple, common, and convenient.

- A gift of cash aids the charity in reaching philanthropic and humanitarian goals.

Tips:

- Save all receipts and bank records for tax purposes.

- Use a credit or debit card and make an immediate or automatic and recurring gift on most charities' websites.

- A gift of cash is considered transferred on the date it is hand-delivered or mailed to the charity. For example: a year-end gift, not received by the charity until January, is still deductible for the prior year if it is postmarked by December 31.

A GIFT OF SECURITIES

Securities are instruments that evidence the holder's ownership rights in a firm (a stock), the holder's creditor relationship with a firm or government (a bond), or the holder's other rights (an option). [5]

Plan a Gift:

---

[4] Gifts of Cash, the Sharpe Group, Inc., http://stcl.givingplan.net/pp/general-information/3061.

[5] Black's Law Dictionary 1559 (10th ed. 2014).

- Transfer securities to a charity.

- The easiest way to transfer securities to a charity is by a letter of instruction to the donor's securities broker requesting a transfer of securities to a charity with the following information (provided by the charity).   Charity's:

  - Brokerage Account Number

  - Depository Trust Corporation Number (DTC): The DTC is the principal central clearing agency for securities transactions of the public markets. [6]

  - Tax ID Number

  - Broker Contact and Address

  - Broker Telephone

Include in the letter of instruction:

  - Donor's name, address, and phone number

  - Name and ticker symbol of the security

  - Number of shares the donor is gifting

  - Purpose or designation of gift (a gift may be designated by a donor for a charity's specific program, or it may be undesignated, making it available for the charity's most pressing needs)

---

[6] Black's Law Dictionary 534 (10th ed. 2014).

DATE:

TO: YOUR BROKERAGE FIRM
FROM: YOUR NAME, ADDRESS, AND PHONE NUMBER

PLEASE TRANSFER (AMOUNT OF SHARES) OF
(NAME AND SYMBOL) STOCK FROM BROKERAGE ACCOUNT
NUMBER_____.

TRANSFER TO:

CHARITY'S BROKERAGE ACCOUNT:
NAME OF CHARITY_____
CHARITY'S BROKERAGE ACCOUNT NUMBER_____
CHARITY'S DTC NUMBER_____
CHARITY'S TAX ID NUMBER_____

CHARITY'S BROKERAGE INFORMATION:
NAME AND ADDRESS_____
BROKER PHONE NUMBER_____

PLEASE CONTACT ME WITH ANY QUESTIONS

THANK YOU,

A WONDERFUL DONOR

DONOR'S NAME
ADDRESS
PHONE NUMBER

Benefits to a Donor:

- A gift of appreciated securities is simple, common, and convenient.

- A charitable deduction may reduce a donor's taxable income (as allowed by law).

- The full market value of the securities is eligible for a charitable deduction up to 30% of adjusted gross income (AGI) in a given year.

- If charitable gifts exceed the 30% deduction amount, the donor may carry the excess deduction on their income tax returns for up to five additional years if eligible.

- A donor may avoid paying capital gains tax on the transfer of appreciated securities to a charity.

- For higher income taxpayers, the itemized deduction phase-out may occur, but state taxes, mortgage interest, and other common deductions will normally absorb these reductions whether or not charitable gifts are made.[7]

- The higher the donor's tax rate, the more the donor will usually save from a charitable deduction.

---

[7] Gifts of Cash, the Sharpe Group, Inc., http://stcl.givingplan.net/pp/general-information/3061.

⚠ **Note:** If an asset has little appreciation and the donor itemizes deductions on a tax return (for example, does not take the standard deduction), it may be best to base a tax deduction on the cost basis of the security and elect to take a 50% deduction of AGI in a given year. A donor may carry the excess deduction on an income tax return up to five additional years if eligible.

But be careful:

Oh No! My securities have decreased in value from my original purchase! Usually a donor will save more in taxes by selling the securities and giving the proceeds (cash) to a charity. In this case, the donor may deduct the value of the cash gift and may also be able to deduct capital losses to offset capital gains realized in the year of the gift. By using this strategy, a donor can gift to charity and may realize greater personal tax savings.

Benefits to a Charity:

- A gift of securities is simple, common, and convenient.

- A gift of securities aids a charity in reaching philanthropic and humanitarian goals.

Tips:

- Stocks, mutual funds, and bonds that have increased in value and have been owned for more than one year provide greater tax benefits to the donor than giving an equivalent amount in cash.[8]

---

[8] For individuals who hold short-term appreciated securities there is little or no tax difference between donating the stock or selling the stock and donating the proceeds.

- If a stock has increased in value and has been owned for more than one year, it may be best to give the stock to charity and at the same time buy back the shares with the cash that otherwise would have been used to make the charitable gift. The basis in the stock will increase to 100% of its current value. Should the donor sell the stock in the future, they could save on capital gains taxes. A donor may also benefit from a loss deduction should the stock decline in value before it is sold.

- Notify the charity prior to every stock transfer. The charity can be on the lookout for the gift, and if the donor wants the funds used for a special purpose, their requests can be considered. Always call a charity if a gift of securities involves special considerations or instructions.

- Electronic transfer information cannot be used for restricted stock or stock traded on non-U.S. markets for making life income gifts, gift annuities, charitable trusts, or transfer of physical stock certificates. Contact a charity for instructions.

- A gift of securities is valued by taking the average of the high and low sales price of the stock or bond on the date of the gift. Because of this averaging, the value of a gift may differ slightly from the actual sale price.

- Save cash for other purposes.

INTANGIBLE PERSONAL PROPERTY

STOCKS

BONDS

LIFE INSURANCE

RETIREMENT PLANS

REAL PROPERTY / REAL ESTATE

TANGIBLE PERSONAL PROPERTY

A GIFT OF PROPERTY

Property is the right to possess and use, the right to exclude, and the right to transfer a tract of land (real estate/real property) and/or personal property.[9]

Real Estate/Real Property is land and anything growing on, attached to, or erected on it, excluding anything that may be severed without injury to the land. Real Estate is also known as real property.[10]

Personal Property is any tangible (having a physical existence) or intangible (lacking a physical existence) property that is subject to ownership and not classified as real property.[11]

Tangible personal property is property that has a physical form and characteristics and can include but not limited to art, books, furniture, and jewelry.[12]

Intangible personal property is property whose value comes from its intangible elements (lacks a physical existence), rather than from its tangible elements (has a physical existence). Examples can include but are not limited to stocks, bonds, stock options, life insurance, annuity contracts, retirement plans, and business goodwill.[13]

---

[9] Black's Law Dictionary 1410 (10th ed. 2014).
[10] Id. at 1412.
[11] Id.
[12] Id.
[13] Id.

REAL PROPERTY / REAL ESTATE

TANGIBLE PERSONAL PROPERTY

Real Estate/Real Property

Real Estate/Real Property is land and anything growing on, attached to or erected on it, excluding anything that may be severed without injury to the land.[14]

🎁 Plan a Gift:

- Contributions of real property represent one of the most complicated yet rewarding opportunities in charitable gift planning.

- Consult the selected charity to determine if a gift of real estate/real property can be used and/or will be accepted by the charity.

Benefits to a Donor:

- A charitable deduction may reduce a donor's taxable income (as allowed by law).

- A donor may avoid capital gains tax on the transfer of appreciated assets to charity.

- There may be a reduction of estate taxes and/or probate costs on a donor's estate.

Benefits to a Charity:

- A gift of real estate/real property aids a charity in reaching philanthropic and humanitarian goals.

---

[14] *Id.*

✅ Tips:

- Gifts of real estate/real property are usually sold by the charity to provide funds for the charity's current needs.

- Check with the charity to determine if a gift of real estate/real property needs to be accompanied by an endowed fund to sustain and maintain the gift. An endowed fund contains assets held and invested by the charity to create an income. If the property is not sold quickly, the endowed fund can be used to provide for the maintenance of the property until the property is sold.

- Gifts of real estate/real property must be appraised by an independent appraiser to determine the value of a charitable deduction.

- Charitable gifts of real estate/real property generally involve more tax and legal complexities than other types of charitable donations but can be very rewarding for the charity and the donor.

- Two key characteristics of gifted property that determine the donor's tax benefits are the length of time the property has been owned and whether it has increased or decreased in value.

Remainder Interest in Real Estate

A Remainder Interest in Real Estate is defined as property that passes to a beneficiary after the expiration of an intervening income interest.[15] A donor can gift a primary residence, vacation home, or certain farm properties to a charity while continuing to enjoy its use (with full rights and responsibilities of the property) for the remainder of a donor's lifetime or a period of time established and agreed upon. A donor continues to maintain the property, pay the taxes, and even receive any income the property generates during this time.

---

[15] Black's Law Dictionary 1484 (10th ed. 2014).

Benefits to a Donor:

- An immediate income tax charitable deduction may reduce a donor's taxable income (as allowed by law).

- A charitable deduction may serve to reduce federal income taxes for the year of the gift and a donor may carry the excess deductions on income tax returns up to five additional tax years if eligible.

- Capital gains tax may be avoided on the transfer of appreciated assets to a charity.

- There may be a reduction of estate taxes and/or probate costs on a donor's estate.

Benefits to a Charity:

- A gift of a remainder interest in real estate/real property aids a charity in reaching philanthropic and humanitarian goals.

Tips:

- The donor continues to maintain the property, pay the taxes, and receive any income the property generates during this time.

- The donor's estate can avoid the expense and delay of probate when a donor makes an irrevocable gift to charity.

18

Personal Property

Tangible Property

Tangible personal property is property that has a physical form and characteristics and can include, but is not limited to, art, books, furniture, and jewelry.

Plan a Gift:

- Before gifting tangible personal property, confirm with the charity that they will accept the offered gift and the gift will be used as the donor wishes.

- If a gift is valued at more than $5,000, the donor must have it appraised by an independent appraiser to determine the donor's charitable deduction.

- A charity is not permitted to assign a value to a gift of tangible personal property.

- Use IRS Form 8283 to document your gift.[16]

---

[16] Form 8283-Noncash- Charitable- Contributions, www.irs.gov.

Charitable Gifts of Tangible Personal Property <u>Related</u> and <u>Not Related</u> to a Charity's Purpose

Gifts <u>related</u> to a charity's purpose:

- Gifts of tangible personal property (related to a charity's purpose) entitles a donor to a deduction (as allowed by law) of the property's full fair market value up to 30% of adjusted gross income as long as the property is held for more than one year.

- A donor may carry the excess deduction on their income tax returns up to five additional tax years if eligible.

Gifts <u>not related</u> to a charity's purpose

- Gifts of tangible personal property (not related to a charity's purpose) entitles a donor to a deduction (as allowed by law) equal to donor's cost basis in the property or its fair market value, whichever is less, up to 50% of adjusted gross income and held for more than one year.

- A donor may carry the excess deduction on their income tax returns up to five additional tax years if eligible.

Intangible Personal Property

Intangible personal property is property whose value comes from its intangible elements (lacks a physical existence) rather than from its tangible elements (has a physical existence).   This section's focus is on life insurance and retirement plan accounts, but note, all personal property should be considered as a possible gift to charity.

LIFE INSURANCE AND RETIREMENT PLAN ACCOUNTS

Often large cash balances are held in life insurance policies and/or retirement plan accounts (such as 401(k)s, 403(b)s, and IRAs.) Many times, these assets are in excess of what a donor needs to meet their retirement income needs. Intangible personal property, such as life insurance and retirement plan accounts, can be a great way to make a gift to a charity. The donor may receive an income tax deduction (as allowed by law) and the charitable gift may reduce estate taxes and/or probate costs on the donor's estate.

LOVING HANDS HOMELESS SHELTER

IN MEMORIAM

CHARITY RECEIVES A LIFE INSURANCE POLICY FROM A DONOR TO CONTINUE ITS PHILANTHROPIC MISSION.

Life Insurance

Life insurance is an agreement between an insurance company and a policy holder to pay a specified amount to a designated beneficiary (in our case, a charity) on the insured's death.
By simply naming a charity or charities as the beneficiary of a new or existing life insurance policy, the charity MAY receive a larger gift than if other assets were gifted.

Plan a Gift:

- Changing the beneficiary on an existing life insurance policy is a simple process. Contact the insurance company professional on your policy for a beneficiary change form.

- A charity can be named as a beneficiary of a life insurance policy by naming them as a:

    o Primary beneficiary—a charity can be the sole beneficiary of a policy.

    o Co-beneficiary—a charity can share in the proceeds with another charity or with others.

    o Contingent beneficiary—a charity receives the proceeds only if one or more other beneficiaries have already passed away.

Benefits to a Donor:

- By gifting a life insurance policy to a charity, a donor may receive considerable income, estate, and gift tax savings.

- A gift of a life insurance policy is not subject to the probate process and cost and is not a matter of public record.

Benefits to a Charity:

- Typically, charitable gifts of life insurance proceeds are larger than the average charitable gift.

- Life insurance proceeds are not subject to the probate process and costs.

- The charity may receive a larger gift more quickly and the proceeds can be put to work immediately.

✔ Tips:

- The fair market value of a life insurance policy is not necessarily the amount the donor can claim as an income tax charitable deduction, but it is the starting point to determine the charitable deduction. Check with an independent counsel to determine the charitable deduction.

- A life insurance contract is NOT SUBJECT to the probate process and costs and IS NOT a matter of public record; a bequest in a will IS SUBJECT to the probate process and costs and IS a matter of public record.

- Probate is the process of proving through the court that a will is valid and both the process and the will itself become matters of public record.

A CHARITY RECEIVES A RETIREMENT PLAN FROM A DONOR TO CONTINUE ITS PHILANTHROPIC MISSION.

Retirement Plans

Many Americans have taken advantage of tax incentives provided by Congress to promote saving for retirement through contributions to their retirement plan accounts—401(k)s, 403(b)s, IRAs, and similar plans.

Your retirement plan account can be a convenient tool from which to make charitable gifts each year.

Plan a Gift:

- Always seek assistance from an independent counsel when determining the optimal amount to gift from retirement plan accounts under current federal and state tax laws.

Benefits to a Donor:

- An income tax charitable deduction (as allowed by law) may reduce your taxable income in the year of the gift. The charitable deduction in the year of the gift may be up to 50% of adjusted gross income (AGI).

- A donor may carry the excess deduction on their income tax returns up to five additional tax years if eligible.

- Gifted retirement plan assets may, in effect, never be subject to gift, income, estate taxes, or probate costs.

Benefits to a Charity:

- A gift from a retirement plan account aids a charity in reaching philanthropic and humanitarian goals.

Tips:

- Retirement plan assets can be a convenient and easy way to make charitable gifts each year.

- Donors over the age of 59½ are eligible to make withdrawals from their IRA or other tax-favored retirement plan accounts without triggering an early withdrawal penalty.

- Income tax will be due on the withdrawal, but if you are able to deduct the full amount of the gift/withdrawal, this may amount to a "wash" for federal tax purposes.

Qualified IRA Charitable Distributions (if legislation passed in current year)

Over 70 ½?

For those over age 70½, it may be possible to make tax-favored charitable gifts from traditional and Roth IRA accounts if current law allows.

A total up to $100,000 may be transferred directly from traditional or Roth IRAs to a 501(c)(3) (charity) free of federal income tax. State income tax savings and/or fulfillment of a Required Minimum Distribution (RMD) of an IRA may be realized.

To make a Qualified IRA Charitable Distribution, it is important not to withdraw funds prior to a gift, but distribute them directly from an IRA to one or more qualified charities. For those with check writing privileges on their accounts, this may be the most efficient way to make gifts directly from an IRA.

Consult with your IRA administrator or your legal, tax, or financial advisor for more information on current tax law.

Qualified IRA Charitable Distributions vs. Regular IRA Charitable Contributions

Qualified IRA Charitable Distributions

- Not added to donor's income
- No charitable deduction

Regular IRA Charitable Contributions

- IRA distribution added to donor's income
- Charitable deductions may be limited or if donor takes the standard deduction, a charitable deduction is not allowed.

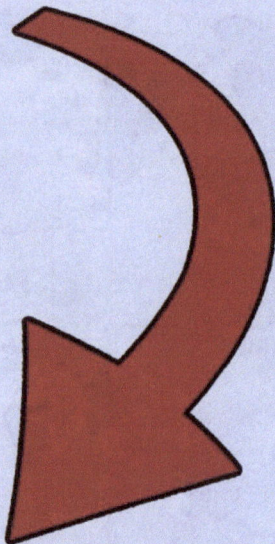

Avoid Double Taxation

Retirement plan assets inherited by heirs may be reduced by a combination of estate and income taxes. Non-charitable organization beneficiaries may be liable for payment of estate taxes up to 40% or more. Income tax will also be due—up to 39.6% or more—depending on state income taxes and other factors.

- The combination of income and estate taxes on retirement plan accounts may, in some cases, amount to the bulk of an account's value.

- Consider gifting retirement plan assets to charity and gifting nonretirement plan assets to heirs.

BEQUESTS

Bank and Investment Accounts

Many people have bank and investment accounts not needed that they would like to leave directly (not in a will) to beneficiaries, including charities, at the end of their lifetime.

Plan a Gift:

- "Pay on death" (P.O.D.) provision for a bank account or a CD or "transfer on death" (T.O.D.) provision for certain other investment accounts are available in order to leave bank and investment accounts directly to a beneficiary.[17]

- Contact the bank manager or financial advisor for advice and the appropriate forms.

Benefits to a Donor:

- The assets given to charity will, in effect, never be subject to gift, income, estate taxes, or probate costs.

- The donor retains full ownership and access to the funds during their lifetime.

- The person or charity receives the remainder in the account at the owner's death according to the donor's plans.

---

[17] Sharpe Group, http://stcl.givingplan.net/pp/giving-through-will-living-trust-and-other-plans/3118.

🤲 **Benefits to a Charity:**

- A gift from a P.O.D. or a T.O.D. account aids a charity in reaching philanthropic and humanitarian goals.

- P.O.D. and T.O.D. charitable gifts are not subject to the probate process and cost, which may mean a larger and immediate gift to charity.

✔️ **Tips:**

- Contact the bank manager or financial advisor for advice and the appropriate forms.

A Bequest through a Will and a Revocable Living Trust

A will is a document by which a person directs his or her estate to be distributed upon death.[18]

A bequest is an act of giving property, usually personal property, by a will.[19]

A charitable bequest is an act of giving property to a philanthropic organization.[20]

---

[18] Black's Law Dictionary 1833 (10th ed. 2014).

[19] *Id.* at 189.

[20] *Id.*

Wills

- **Both large and small bequests play a major role in the development and success of charities. A bequest can be included in the body of your will or in an addition to it (a codicil).**

Types of Bequests include but are not limited to:

- **Residuary Bequest—all or portions of an estate that may be given to a beneficiary (charity) after specific amounts or assets are distributed to other beneficiaries.**

- **Specific Bequest—a certain percentage of an estate, a certain dollar amount, or particular securities or assets that may be given to a beneficiary (charity).**

Plan a Gift:

- Contact an independent counsel and discuss your interest in making a bequest to a charity. To name a charity as a beneficiary, use its legal name and make sure all identifying information is correct. The following is recommended bequest language:

"After fulfilling all other provisions, I give, devise, and bequeath ___% of the remainder of my estate or trust [or $___, if a specific amount] to (Name of Charity)_____ [Tax ID Number]_____, a charitable organization incorporated under the laws of (state)____, and presently having offices at (address)_____"

Benefits to a Donor:

- There are no charitable deduction limits (no tax due) for federal gift and estate taxes for charitable gifts made by a will or a trust.[21]

- The donor has arranged a gift for a charity during their lifetime.

- The donor can make a larger gift at death without using needed lifetime assets.

- The donor may revise a will at any time if there is a change of heart or financial circumstance.

Benefits to a Charity:

- A gift from a will or trust aids a charity in reaching philanthropic and humanitarian goals.

- The charity may receive a larger gift from a will than the donor was able to give during their lifetime.

---

[21] The Sharpe Group, http://stcl.givingplan.net/pp/giving-through-will-living-trust-and-other-plans/3118.

✓ Tips:

- Remember that wills are subject to the probate process and costs and are a matter of public record.

- *Check with an independent counsel if any assets named in a will could by-pass the probate process using another estate planning vehicle. This can include but is not limited to trusts, life insurance contracts, retirement plans, P.O.D., and T.O.D. accounts.*

SUPPORT YOUR LOCAL CHARITY THROUGH YOUR REVOCABLE LIVING TRUST.

A trust establishes the right, solely enforceable in equity, to the beneficial enjoyment of property to which another person holds the legal title; the property interest is held by one person (the trustee) at the request of another (the settlor) for the benefit of a third party (the beneficiary). For the trust to be valid, it must involve specific property, reflect the settlor's intent, and be created for a lawful purpose. The two primary types of trusts are private and charitable trusts.[22]

A private trust is a trust created for the financial benefit of one or more individuals, not for the public benefit; whereas a charitable trust is created for the public benefit, for example a charity.

A revocable trust is a trust in which the settlor reserves the right to terminate the trust and recover the trust property and any undistributed income.[23]

A living trust is a trust that is created and takes effect during the settlor's lifetime.[24]

A revocable living trust is a trust that is created and becomes effective during a settlor's (a person who creates or transfers property to a trust) lifetime. The settlor reserves the right to terminate the trust and recover the trust property and any undistributed income.[25]

Plan a Gift:

- Consult an independent counsel who specializes in the area of revocable living trusts.

---

[22] *Id.* at 1740.
[23] *Id.* at 1746.
[24] *Id.*
[25] *Id.*

Benefits to a Donor:

- The income earned by a living trust may be paid to the donor, charity, or others.

- The income paid to a charity is tax deductible.

- A living trust avoids the probate process and its costs.

- The donor reserves the right to change or terminate the trust and recover the trust property.

- The donor has an opportunity to use professional management of assets in the trust.

- The donor may make a larger charitable gift from a trust than they were able to do during their lifetime.

Benefits to a Charity:

- A gift from a revocable living trust aids a charity in reaching philanthropic and humanitarian goals.

- A charity may receive a larger gift from a revocable living trust than the donor was able to give during their lifetime.

- A charitable gift from a revocable living trust is not subject to the probate process and costs, which may mean a larger and immediate gift to a charity.

✔ Tips:

- There are no income tax benefits to a revocable living trust unless the income of the trust is paid to a charity.

- An estate tax deduction from a revocable living trust is allowed only if property passes to a charity.

CHARITABLE GIFT ANNUITY

3 DONOR RECEIVES AN INCOME FOR LIFE

2 THE DONOR RECEIVES AN INCOME TAX DEDUCTION AS ALLOWED BY LAW

4 At THE END OF THE ANNUITY PERIOD, THE CHARITY RECEIVES THE GIFT TO FURTHER ITS MISSION

1 DONOR TRANSFER ASSETS TO A CHARITY IN EXCHANGE FOR A CHARITABLE GIFT ANNUITY

CHARITABLE GIFT ANNUITIES AND CHARITABLE TRUSTS

Charitable gift annuities (CGA) and charitable trusts provide significant benefits to a charity as well as to a donor.

Charitable Gift Annuities/Fixed Lifetime Income Payments

A charitable gift annuity (CGA) is a contract between a donor and a charity. The donor makes an irrevocable gift to charity and in return receives fixed lifetime income payments.

Plan a Gift:

- A donor can irrevocably transfer cash or other assets to a charity in exchange for fixed lifetime income payments.

- Contact the charity for age minimums, rates, and minimum funding for a charitable gift annuity.

- Additions may not be made to a gift annuity, but more than one gift annuity may be established.

Benefits to a Donor:

- A donor can receive fixed lifetime income payments for self, spouse, and/or other individual.

- *An increase in income may be available from a charitable gift annuity when transferring assets from low-yielding stocks, bonds, or other assets.*

- A donor may receive an immediate income tax deduction (as allowed by law) based on the amount of the charitable gift annuity, the ages of the income beneficiaries, and the income amount received.

- Part of each income payment is tax free for a period of time and part is ordinary income. If the annuity is funded with appreciated securities, part is treated as capital gains income. The assets used to fund a gift annuity will generally be removed from an estate for probate and tax purposes.

Benefits to a Charity:

- The gift proceeds from a charitable gift annuity are irrevocable.

- The gift proceeds from a charitable gift annuity avoid the probate process and costs.

Tips:

- The lifetime fixed income payments can be paid annually (or more frequently, if desired).

- The charitable gift annuity payments will not change with interest rate and investment market fluctuations.

- The donor can choose to name another person (often a spouse, parent, or sibling) to receive payments with the donor, instead of the donor, or following the donor's lifetime for the remainder of their life.

- Charitable gift annuities are easy to create and can be funded with gifts of relatively modest amounts.

- A donor may choose to fund more than one gift annuity over time. Because payment rates may increase with age, each gift annuity of an equal amount generally features larger payments.

- When appreciated property such as stock, mutual funds, or other securities are given for a charitable gift annuity, the charitable deduction can be based on the full value of the property, not just its original cost.

Deferred Charitable Gift Annuities

Deferred Charitable Gift Annuities: A donor may defer income (that begins at least one year after the gift annuity is funded) from a charitable gift annuity and enjoy larger payments that begin later. This is called a Deferred Charitable Gift Annuity and receives an immediate income tax deduction (as allowed by law).

Charitable Gift Annuity Rates are determined by the American Council on Gift Annuities (ACGA).

The American Council on Gift Annuities (formerly the Committee on Gift Annuities) was formed in 1927 "to study and recommend the proper range of rates, the forms of contracts, the amount and type of reserve funds and the nomenclature to be used, to ascertain and advise as to the legislation in the United States and the various states regarding [charitable gift] annuities, their taxability, etc." to better assure the donor's focus was on the charitable cause(s) to be supported by their gift, rather than the gift annuity payment rate being offered by charities competing for the gift. The first suggested gift annuity payout rates were adopted at the first Conference on Gift Annuities in April 1927. The ACGA actively promotes responsible philanthropy through actuarially sound charitable gift annuity rate recommendations, quality training opportunities and the advocacy of appropriate consumer protection. One of the primary activities of the Council is the publication of suggested charitable gift annuity rates for use by charities and their donors. The Council retains the services of an actuarial firm to advise and consult on matters pertaining to life expectancies and related matters. The Council has a long and distinguished record in this area, and its suggested rates have long been recognized, not only by charities and donors, but also by state insurance departments and the IRS as being actuarially sound and in the best interests of all parties involved. ACGA offers a conference every two years, for planned giving, development and administrative staff of non-profits and related professionals.

The Council's volunteer board of directors is comprised of professionals active in the field of planned giving with some of America's most well-respected charities. These individuals give unselfishly of their time and energy to assist others in their gift annuity programs.[26]

---

[26] American Council on Gift Annuities (ACGA), http://www.acga-web.org/.

Charitable Trusts

The two primary types of trusts are private trusts and charitable trusts.

This section will focus on charitable trusts.   Charitable trusts are trusts created to benefit a specific charity, specific charities, or the general public rather than a private individual or entity.[27] A charitable trust offers a way to make future gifts for philanthropic purposes after first providing income for a donor and others named in the trust.

Charitable Trusts are often eligible for tax-favored treatment.[28]

There are two types of charitable trusts: charitable remainder trusts and charitable lead trusts.

---

[27] Black's Law Dictionary 1741 (10th ed. 2014).
[28] Id.

Charitable Remainder Trust (CRT)

A charitable remainder trust is a popular estate planning strategy for the wealthy, but it is also excellent for people who find themselves with large amounts of money due to an inheritance, life insurance proceeds, or appreciated assets/investments. A CRT allows a person to give more money to charity, retain an interest income for themselves and their family, and get a significant tax deduction. The term of the trust is generally for the life of the donor, or a term of years (not to exceed 20). At the end of either situation, the balance goes to charity.[29]

There are two types of charitable remainder trusts.

A charitable remainder annuity trust (CRAT) provides a donor with a level and predictable income.

A charitable remainder unitrust (CRUT) provides a donor with a variable income.

Charitable Remainder Annuity Trust (CRAT) – Predictable Income

Charitable Remainder Annuity Trust (CRAT) provides predictable income.

🎁 Plan a Gift:

- Consult an independent counsel who specializes in the area of charitable trusts to advise you and to draft a trust document.

- Clearly state your intentions and terms in the trust document.

- Choose a trustee and clearly state your intentions and terms to them.

---

[29] The Sharpe Group, http://stcl.givingplan.net/pp/charitable-trusts-help-you-reach-many-goals/3144.

- Once the trust is in place, it is an irrevocable instrument.

- Assets are transferred to the trust to be managed by the donor, another person, or entity chosen by a trustee.

- Determine the annual payment percentage when the trust is drafted. Each year, the percentage (at least 5%) of the initial trust assets' value is paid to the donor or others named in the trust.

- Payments are made from the trust to a donor and/or others the donor name for life, or other period of time donor determines (not to exceed 20 years).

- When the trust terminates, its remaining assets become a charitable gift to one or more charitable interests named in the trust.

- The charitable gift portion is known as the charitable remainder.

Benefits to a Donor:

- A donor can receive fixed annual income for life or term of years (not to exceed 20).

- The charitable gift will result in an immediate charitable income tax deduction (as allowed by law) for a portion of the assets' value placed in the trust.

- Capital gains tax is by-passed in the year the trust is created.

- Amounts used to fund the trust may not be part of a probate or taxable estate.

- The value of the trust assets at death generally is deductible from a donor's estate for tax purposes.

Benefits to a Charity:

- A gift from a charitable remainder annuity trust aids a charity in reaching its philanthropic and humanitarian goals.

- A charitable gift from a CRAT is not subject to the probate process and costs, which may mean an immediate and larger gift to a charity.

- The awareness of an impending charitable gift (when the trust terminates) helps the charity plan for its future.

✔ Tips:

- The value of the assets expected to be received by the charity is determined by IRS code 7520.[30]

- A CRAT is a way to make a charitable gift while assuring a fixed, regular reliable income to supplement a retirement income.

- Income payments received each year must be at least 5% of the amount originally placed in the trust and will be determined when the trust is created.

- A CRAT may be created for a term-of-years (not to exceed 20) in order to provide income for short-term needs.

---

[30] Internal Revenue Code 7520 is used to value certain charitable interests in trusts. Pursuant to Internal Revenue Code 7520, the interest rate for a particular month is 120 percent of the applicable federal midterm rate (compounded annually) for the month in which the valuation date falls. That rate is then rounded to the nearest two-tenths of one percent. www.IRS.gov.

CHARITABLE REMAINDER UNITRUST

It grows with you

Charitable Remainder Unitrust (CRUT) – Variable Income

A charitable remainder unitrust (CRUT) provides variable income.

Like the charitable remainder annuity trust (CRAT), the charitable remainder unitrust (CRUT) allows a donor to retain income for life or other period of time the donor chooses (not to exceed 20 years). Keep in mind that the charitable remainder annuity trust (CRAT) provides predicable income and the charitable remainder unitrust (CRUT) provides income that can fluctuate over time with the value of the assets placed in the trust. The CRUT can be an attractive option for those who want to provide for income that can grow over time.

Plan a Gift:

- Consult an independent counsel who specializes in the area of charitable trusts to advise you and to draft a trust document.

- Clearly state your intentions and terms in the trust document.

- Choose a trustee and clearly state your intentions and terms to them.

- Once the trust is in place, it is an irrevocable instrument.

- Assets are transferred to the trust to be managed by the donor, another person, or an entity chosen as trustee.

- Determine the annual payment percentage when the gift is made. Each year the percentage (at least 5%) of the value of the trust assets is paid to the donor or others named in the trust.

- The income will be more if the value of the assets increase.

- The income will be less if the value of the assets decrease.

- If provided for in the trust agreement, additions can be made to a unitrust and an additional tax deduction is allowed for part of any additional amounts contributed.

- Payments are made from the trust to the donor and/or others the donor names for life or other period of time the donor determines (not to exceed 20 years).

- When the trust ends, its remaining assets become a gift to one or more charitable interests named in the trust.

- The gift portion is known as the charitable remainder.

Benefits to a Donor:

- The donor and/or beneficiaries receive a variable annual income.

- The donor receives an immediate charitable income tax deduction (as allowed by law) for a portion of assets placed in the trust.

- The donor's capital gains tax is bypassed at the time the trust is funded.

- The trust assets at death are generally deductible from the donor's estate for tax purposes.

Benefits to a Charity:

- A gift from a charitable remainder unitrust aids a charity in reaching its philanthropic and humanitarian goals.

- The gift proceeds from a charitable remainder unitrust are immediate upon trust termination and avoid the probate process and costs.

- The awareness of an impending charitable gift (when the trust terminates) helps the charity plan for its future.

Tips:

- Even if the charity does not receive any benefit for several decades, it will eventually receive its share of the trust remainder.

- The trustee controls the assets in the trust.

- The trustee should know how to handle financial matters and be willing to carry out the donor's intentions.

- The rate of income is defined in the trust agreement (at least 5% of trust assets).

- The value of the assets expected to be received by the charity is determined by IRS code 7520.[31]

Charitable Remainder Trust for a Term of Years

A term-of–years trust is a type of annuity trust (CRAT) (fixed income) or unitrust (CRUT) (variable income) that pays income over a specified period of years (not to exceed 20) rather than over a lifetime.

---

[31] Internal Revenue Code 7520 is used to value certain charitable interests in trusts. Pursuant to Internal Revenue Code 7520, the interest rate for a particular month is 120 percent of the applicable federal midterm rate (compounded annually) for the month in which the valuation date falls. That rate is then rounded to the nearest two-tenths of one percent. www.IRS.gov.

CHARITABLE LEAD TRUST FOR A TERM OF YEARS.

Charitable Lead Trust (CLT)

A Charitable Lead Trust (CLT) is an irrevocable trust, which initially makes payments to a charity for a specified term. The trustor or other named person(s) receives the property after the term expires.

Plan a Gift:

- Consult an independent counsel who specializes in the area of charitable trusts to advise you and to draft a trust document.

- Contact an independent counsel to draft a trust document.

- Clearly state your intentions and terms in the trust document.

- Choose a trustee and clearly state your intentions and terms to them.

- Transfer assets to the trust to be managed by the donor, another person, or an entity chosen to be trustee.

- Once the trust is in place, it is an irrevocable instrument.

- Arrange for immediate charitable gifts that will continue for as long as the donor decides.

Benefits to a Donor:

- Either fixed or variable payments can be made from the trust for a period of time the donor determines.

- At the end of that time period, the assets remaining in the trust are returned to the donor or others the donor designates.

- Depending on the amount of the charitable payments, how long they last, and other factors, it can be possible to reduce, or even eliminate entirely, gift and estate tax on unlimited amounts ultimately passing to heirs.

Benefits to a Charity:

- Unlike a charitable remainder trust (CRT), under the terms of a charitable lead trust (CLT), charitable interests immediately begin to receive gifts in the form of payments from the trust.

- The charity can receive immediate income from the trust property for a fixed period to aid them in reaching their philanthropic and humanitarian goals, after which the trust property reverts back to the settlor's estate.

Tips:

- With a charitable lead trust, a donor makes a gift to a charity for a term of years. After the term is completed, the assets may be passed to heirs or to the donor's estate in a cost effective way.

- With charitable lead trust gifts, heirs may receive a larger inheritance at a later time when it is more appropriate for them to inherit the trust's assets.

- Charitable lead trusts are especially attractive during times when interest rates are low and when assets used to fund them are expected to grow over time.

- Lead trusts can serve to reduce or eliminate income, estate, and gift taxes now and in future years as well.

CHARITABLE CONTRIBUTIONS/INTERNAL REVENUE SERVICE

Note:

Topic 506 - Charitable Contributions

Charitable contributions are deductible only if you itemize deductions on <u>Form 1040, Schedule A</u>.

To be deductible, charitable contributions must be made to qualified organizations. Payments to individuals are never deductible. See <u>Publication 526</u>, Charitable Contributions. To determine if the organization that you have contributed to qualifies as a charitable organization for income tax deductions, review <u>Exempt Organizations</u> on the IRS.gov website.

If your contribution entitles you to merchandise, goods, or services, including admission to a charity ball, banquet, theatrical performance, or sporting event, you can deduct only the amount that exceeds the fair market value of the benefit received.

For a contribution of cash, check, or other monetary gift (regardless of amount), you must maintain as a record of the contribution a bank record or a written communication from the qualified organization containing the name of the organization, the date of the contribution, and the amount of the contribution. In addition to deducting your cash contributions, you generally can deduct the fair market value of any other property you donate to qualified organizations. See <u>Publication 561</u>, Determining the Value of Donated Property. For any contribution of $250 or more (including contributions of cash or property), you must obtain and keep in your records a contemporaneous written acknowledgment from the qualified organization indicating the amount of the cash and a description of any property contributed. The acknowledgment must say whether the organization provided any goods or services in exchange for the gift and, if so, must provide a description and a good faith estimate of the value of those goods or services. One document from the qualified organization may satisfy both the written communication requirement for monetary gifts and the contemporaneous written acknowledgment requirement for all contributions of $250 or more.

You must fill out Form 8283 (PDF), and attach it to your return, if your deduction for a noncash contribution is more than $500. If you claim a deduction for a contribution of noncash property worth $5,000 or less, you must fill out Form 8283, Section A. If you claim a deduction for a contribution of noncash property worth more than $5,000, you will need a qualified appraisal of the noncash property and must fill out Form 8283, Section B. If you claim a deduction for a contribution of noncash property worth more than $500,000, you also will need to attach the qualified appraisal to your return.

Special rules apply to donations of certain types of property such as automobiles, inventory and investments that have appreciated in value. For more information, refer to Publication 526, Charitable Contributions. For information on determining the value of your noncash contributions, refer to Publication 561, determining the Value of Donated Property.[32]

---

[32] Topic 506 - Charitable Contributions, http://www.irs.gov/taxtopics/tc506.html.

DISCLOSURE

This book does not provide legal, tax, or financial planning advice. The information and illustrations in this book are for educational purposes only. The type of assets transferred, the actual date of the gift, IRS codes, and other factors may have a material effect on the amount or use of a charitable gift and tax deduction. It is always advisable to seek the advice of independent legal, tax, and/or financial counsel who specialize in charitable giving. An independent counsel gives assistance that is impartial and not given to further the interest of the person giving the advice.

CHARITABLE GIVING TERMS & DEFINITIONS

- **Actuarial tables** — mortality tables used to calculate life expectancy for people in various categories, for example age and gender.

- **Adjusted gross income (AGI)** — gross income minus allowable deductions written in the tax code.

- **Administration** — management and executive duties of a charity.

- **Annuitant** — person receiving payments from a gift annuity.

- **Appraisal** — assessment of what constitutes a fair price, value, or worth.

- **Appreciated property** — asset (property) that has increased in value since purchase.

- **Asset** — an item that is owned and has value.

- **Basis**—a value assigned to an investment in a property and used primarily to calculate a gain or loss.

- **Bequest** — gift of property that the owner passes to another person at death.

- **Broker** — person engaged in the business of conducting securities transactions for the accounts of others.

- **Brokerage** — business of a broker.

- **Capital gains** — profit realized when a capital asset is sold or exchanged.

- **Carryover provision** — if more than the deductible limit is gifted in one year, excess deductions may be carried forward up to an additional five years, if eligible.

- Cash — money or its equivalent — cash includes paper currency, coins, negotiable checks, balances in bank accounts, electronic funds transfers, and debit and credit card transactions.

- Cash surrender value — amount of money the policy owner receives from a life insurance company if the owner cashes in the policy prior to the maturity date (death of insured).

- Charitable deduction — amount of money a person may deduct from his/her federal income tax return for a gift to a qualified charity (as allowed by law).

- Charitable gift — an inter vivos (during lifetime) or testamentary (at death) gift to a qualified charity.

- Charitable gift annuity — contract between a donor and a qualified charity. The donor makes an irrevocable gift to charity and in return receives fixed, lifetime payments.

- Charitable lead trust (CLT) — irrevocable trust, which initially makes payments to a charity for a specified term, with the donor/trustor or other person(s) receiving the property after the trust term expires.

- Charitable remainder annuity trust (CRAT) — irrevocable trust in which trust beneficiaries receive for a specified period 5% or more of the fair market value of the original principle, after which the remaining principle passes to charity. The remaining principal is called the charitable remainder.

- Charitable remainder unitrust (CRUT) — irrevocable trust in which trust beneficiaries receive variable income based on a fixed percentage (at least 5%) of the trust's annual value, after which the remaining principle passes to charity. The remaining principal is called the charitable remainder.

- Charitable trust — trust created to benefit a specific charity or charities or the general public rather than a private individual or entity. Charitable trusts are eligible for favorable tax treatment.

- Charity — goodwill.

- Check — draft signed by a maker, drawn on a bank, and payable on demand.

- Codicil — written and witnessed document that amends an existing will.

- Corpus — amount of assets in a trust or annuity representing the capital distinct from the interest or income.

- Cost basis — original price of an asset plus or minus costs used to determine capital gains. In the case of an inheritance, it is usually the value at the time of the donor's death.

- Credit card — card from a financial institution used to buy items on credit.

- Debit card — card used to pay for purchases by electronic transfer from the purchaser's bank account.

- Deferred gift — gift that is presently made by the donor yet not received by the charity until a later, agreed-upon date.

- Deferred payment gift annuity — gift annuity in which the donor makes an immediate gift to charity but does not begin receiving lifetime payments until a later agreed-upon time set in the agreement-deferred at least one year.

- Disclosure statement — language which explains all material facts of a charitable gift plan.

- Dividend — amount of income (company's earnings or profits) paid each year on a life insurance policy or share of stock.

- Donor— an individual who makes charitable contributions of property to a nonprofit institution.

- Electronic funds transfer — payment of money from one person or entity to another made through a computerized banking system, beginning with originator's payment and ending when final payment is received by beneficiary's bank.

- Endowment — assets held and invested by a charity to create an income for the charity.   A true endowment is restricted by the donor, and such funds may never be used for administration and operations except in fiscal emergencies. A Quasi endowment is set aside at the discretion of the charity's board and may be used at some future date by later board action.

- Estate planning — preparation for the distribution and management of a person's estate at death through the use of wills, trusts, insurance policies, and other arrangements to reduce administration costs and transfer tax-liability. [33]

- Estate tax — tax payable from an estate at death.

- Estate tax deduction for charitable gifts — unlimited deduction (no tax due) for cash or other property given to a qualified charity at death.

- Executor — male named in a will to administer the estate and execute the terms of the will.

- Executrix — female named in a will to administer the estate and execute the terms of the will.

- Fair market value (FMV) — price that a willing buyer would pay a willing seller, neither being under any pressure to buy or sell.

- Fiduciary — acting on a legal and financial matter on behalf of a beneficiary.

- For profit — organization formed for making a profit (difference in earnings over expenses).

- Foundation (charitable) – fund established for benevolent purposes.

- General administrative and operational expense—costs incurred in running a business, includes but not limited to, salaries, mortgage payments, rent, utilities, legal, and accounting services.

---

[33] Black's Law Dictionary 667 (10th ed. 2014).

- **Gift planning (planned giving)** –charitable giving strategy, either during lifetime (inter vivos), or at death (testamentary), from an overall estate or financial plan.

- **Gift tax** — tax due on gifts made by a donor when assets are passed from one person to another. Gift tax is not levied on gifts to charities.

- **Grantor** — trustor, person who creates, and transfers property to a trust.

- **Income beneficiary** — person who receives income from a charitable gift annuity or charitable trust.

- **Independent Counsel** – assistance that is impartial and not given to further the interest of the person giving the advice.

- **Intangible property**—property that lacks a physical existence, includes but not limited to stocks and bonds.

- **Internal Revenue Code 7520**—used to value certain charitable interests in trusts. Pursuant to Internal Revenue Code 7520, the interest rate for a particular month is the rate that is 120 percent of the applicable federal midterm rate (compounded annually) for the month in which the valuation date falls. That rate is then rounded to the nearest two-tenths of one percent.[34]

- **Inter vivos**—property conveyed during a person's lifetime (not through a will).

- **Intestate** — dying without a valid will.

- **Irrevocable** — something which cannot be canceled or reversed.

- **Itemized deduction**— expense (such as a home-mortgage interest, medical expense, or a charitable contribution) that can be subtracted from adjusted gross income to determine taxable income.

---

[34] 7520-Interest-Rates, http://www.irs.gov/Businesses/Small-Businesses-&-Self-Employed/Section-7520-Interest-Rates.

- **Life estate arrangement** — donor deeds his/her home to a charity reserving the right to live on the property for life.

- **Life income gift** — charitable gift that provides income payments to a donor and/or one or more persons for life, for example a charitable gift annuity or charitable trust.

- **Limited Partnership** — partnership composed of one or more persons who control the business and are personally liable for the partnership's debts (general partners) and one or more persons who contribute capital and share profits but who do not manage the business and are liable for only the amount of their contribution to the partnership (limited partners).

- **Listed option** — right (but not the obligation) to buy or sell a given quantity of securities, commodities, or other assets at a fixed price within a specified time.

- **Master Limited Partnership** — limited partnership whose interests or shares are publically traded.

- **Mission** — specific goal.

- **Mutual fund** — Investment Company that invests its shareholders' money usually in a diversified selection of securities (stocks and bonds).

- **Nonprofit Corporation** — organized for some purpose (generally benevolent) rather than making a profit for owners and shareholders. A nonprofit corporation customarily is afforded special tax treatment.

- **Nonprofit status** — state law concept and determined by each individual state — may allow the organization to qualify for benefits at the state level, including exemption from state and local sales, property, and income taxes.

- **Operation** — way things work.

- **Ordinary income** — for individual income tax purposes—money or other forms of compensation you earn from wages, commissions, or interest as opposed to money received from capital gains (profit realized when a capital asset is sold or exchanged).

- Personal property — any tangible (has a physical existence) or intangible (lacks a physical existence) item that is subject to ownership and not classified as real property/real estate.

- Philanthropy — practice of helping others through the generous donation of money and/or property to good causes.

- Planned giving (gift planning) – charitable giving strategy, either during lifetime (inter vivos), or at death (testamentary), from an overall estate or financial plan.

- Probate — proving (through the court) that a will is valid.

- Profit—difference in earnings greater than expenses.

- Property — right to possess and use, the right to exclude, and the right to transfer a tract of land (real estate/real property) or personal property [35]

- Publicly traded securities—common and convenient form of noncash charitable gift assets that are often highly appreciated, easily transferred, and, usually easily valued for charitable deduction purposes without the need for a qualified appraisal.

- Real estate — (real property) land and anything growing on, attached to, or erected on it, excluding anything on it that may be severed without injury to the land.

- Real property (real estate) — land and anything growing on, attached to, or erected on it, excluding anything on it that may be severed without injury to the land.

- Residue — amount left over after designated assets have been distributed in a will.

- Restricted security — security that is not registered with the Securities and Exchange Commission (SEC) and may not be sold

---

[35] Black's Law Dictionary 1410 (10th ed. 2014).

publically unless particular conditions are met.

- Revocable living trust — trust which may be canceled or reversed by settlor/trustor.

- Remainderman (remainder beneficiary) – person or organization entitled to receive the assets of a trust at the death of the settlor/trustor or expiration of a term of years trust.

- Revocable — something which can be canceled or reversed.

- Security — instrument that evidences the holder's ownership rights in a firm (stock), the holder's creditor relationship with a firm or government (bond), or the holder's other rights (option). [36]

- Savings bonds — nontransferable bond issued by the U.S. Government.

- Settlor (grantor, trustor) — person who creates or transfers property to a trust.

- Stock power — power of attorney allowing a person, other than the owner, to transfer ownership of a security to someone else.

- Tangible property — property that has physical form and characteristics, includes, but not limited to art, books, furniture, and jewelry.

- Tax-exempt status — set by the Internal Revenue Service (IRS) under the Internal Revenue Code (IRC) § 501 and is not subject to federal taxation, for example, a tax-exempt charity. Under IRC § 501 (c) (3) charitable contributions to a tax-exempt charity are tax-deductible only if donor itemizes deductions on a tax return. In addition, IRS recognized § 501 (c) (3) organizations have the ability to apply for grants and other public or private allocations.

- Testamentary gift — gift made in a will (at death).

- Testamentary trust — trust created in a person's will.

[36] *Id* at 1559.

- Testator — person making a valid will.

- Trustee — person or entity responsible for administering a trust.

- Will — document, signed and witnessed, of a person's intent to distribute their assets at death.

ABOUT THE AUTHOR

Patricia Guter is an attorney and Certified Financial Planner™. Her expertise is helping individuals, charities, attorneys, and tax and financial professionals with planned giving strategies and techniques to convert assets into charitable gifts.

Patricia has worked with numerous charities as a planned giving officer and has developed planned giving programs in organizations that lacked this form of giving.

She speaks at conferences, sharing her experience and expertise in charitable giving, tax strategies, IRS charitable giving regulations, and planned giving techniques.

Patricia is a member of the American Bar Association, District of Columbia Bar Association, Financial Planning Association, and Planned Giving Association/Partnership for Philanthropic Planning.

www.ingramcontent.com/pod-product-compliance
Lightning Source LLC
Chambersburg PA
CBHW052052190326
41519CB00002BA/191